WHERE'S MY BABY?

Julie Ashworth
John Clark

This book belong's to camille Renaveng!

LONGMAN

Mrs Monster has lost her baby.

POLICE
I've lost my baby. Please help me.

Is this your baby, Mrs Monster?
No, my baby isn't red.

Is this your baby, Mrs Monster?
No, my baby's got one head.

Is this your baby, Mrs Monster?
No, my baby isn't green.

Is this your baby, Mrs Monster?
No, my baby's nice and clean.

Is this your baby, Mrs Monster?
No, my baby's got a nose.

Is this your baby, Mrs Monster?
No, my baby's got ten toes.

Is this your baby, Mrs Monster?
No, my baby isn't hairy.

Is this your baby, Mrs Monster?
No, my baby isn't scary.

There's one more here. But it's a horrible sight.
It's very ugly, bald and white.

That's my baby.
He's called Rick.

Yeuch!
What a monster!
I feel sick!